Shred after Writing

Ali Porter

Hello You!

Hello you! And by this I mean the you that you are meant to be.

In this busy world of over-sharing on social media a 'version' of you, it's time to reawaken and rediscover the **real** you, as if no-one was watching or judging. The you that may have changed over time to fit in to situations life has presented to you. The you that has gradually been erased by the humdrum of the day to day. The you that may be uncomfortable. The you that is caring. The you that may be guarded. The you that is joyous. The you that is hidden from others and most of all, yourself.

This book will question your past, your present and your future, sometimes randomly, sometimes deliberately but, it will give you the opportunity to step out of the shadows, to reveal your light and dark sides. Take your fingers off the like and share buttons, allow your thoughts and maybe even tears to flow, really take the time to reflect on your thoughts, actions and triggers. Be honest with yourself, treat it as a mirror to your inner thoughts and then let that shit go.

It's not a diary, it's not a journal, you can write whenever the mood takes you and when you're done you can keep it, burn it, bury it or shred it, it's totally up to you!

Firsts...

Pet...

School...

Friend...

Best friend...

Hobby...

Party...

Sleepover...

Love...

Kiss...

Fight...

More Firsts...

Performance...

Time I helped a friend...

Song I downloaded...

Live band...

Vacation overseas...

Significant event in history I can remember...

Proud of myself moment...

Time I felt embarrassed...

Item I bought with my own money...

Time I realised I was good at something...

Things I like to do when I feel bored...

My absolute favorite thing to do...

My favorite band and solo artist...

What music makes me particularly happy?

What do I wish I knew how to do, but I can't right now?

Am I more creative or practical?

Do I procrastinate?

Do I feel like I'm being responsible?

My thoughts about bullying...

Have I ever treated anyone badly? What was the situation?

Am I more introvert or extrovert?

How important is family to me?

What do I dream about?

What are my thoughts on marriage?

Is family meal time important to me?

Do my parents embarrass me? If so, how?

Who would be my ideal partner?

What qualities would my ideal partner have?

How would I describe the word 'love' to someone without using the word love?

What does unconditional love mean to me?

Have I ever had my heart broken?

Have I ever broken someone's heart?
Who were they and what was the situation?

Do I think of myself as religious or spiritual?

Do I believe in soul mates and true love?

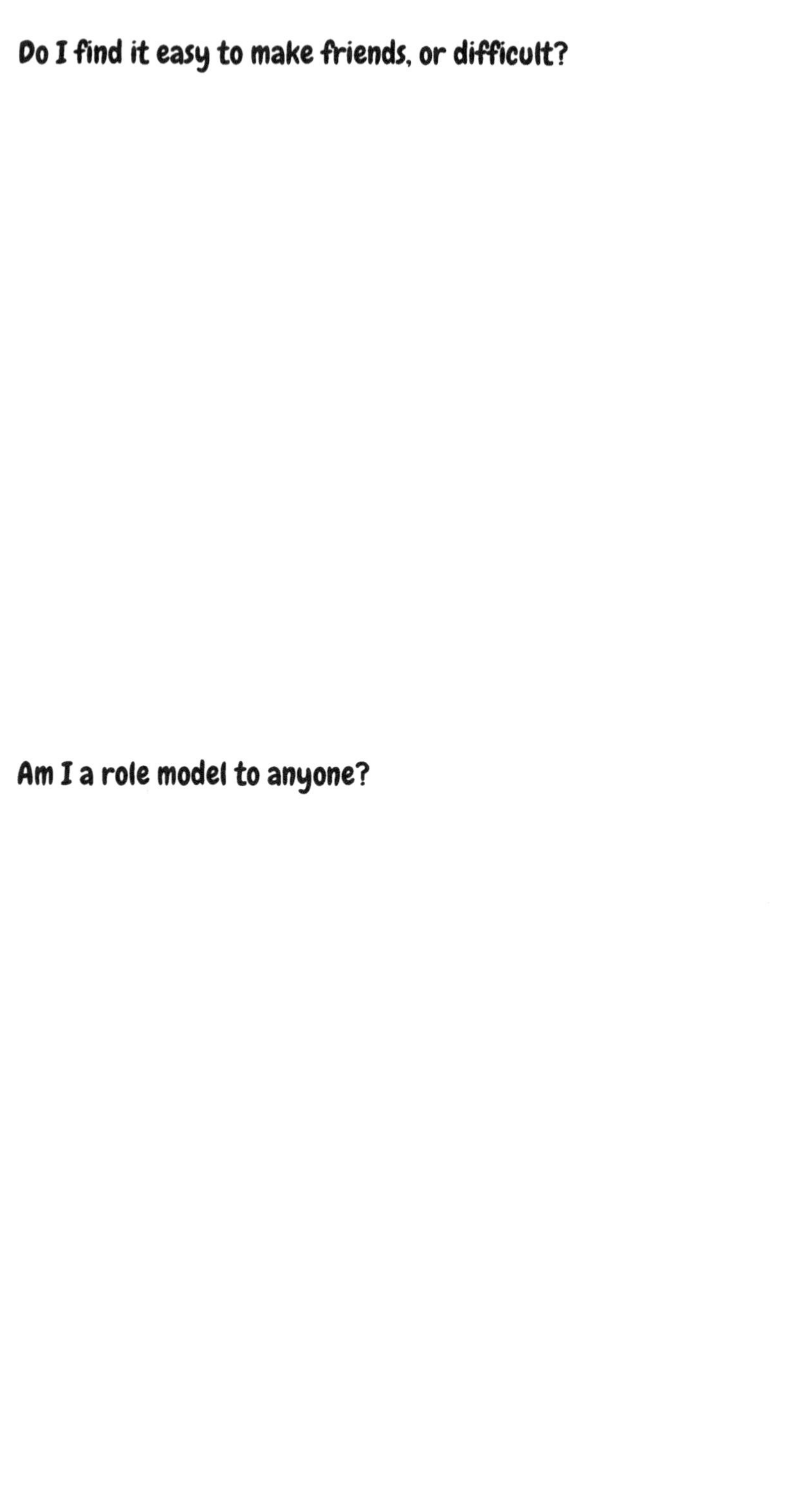
Do I find it easy to make friends, or difficult?
Am I a role model to anyone?

Have I ever been in love with someone and they had no idea?

Has a friend ever been in love with me, but I didn't feel the same way?

Right now I am...

Listening...

Reading...

Making...

Feeling...

Planning...

Loving...

Who knows me the best?

What 3 qualities do I admire in others?
Do I have these qualities myself?

What is my biggest fear?

What is my greatest wish?

What are my top 3 goals for the next 12 months?

How can I work towards my goals?

On a scale of 1-10 how strict are my parents?
Why are they this strict?

What annoys me most about my parents?

What do I wish I knew more about my parents?

Who do I wish I was more like and why?

Do I think I am enough?

How do I handle feeling anxious?

How do I show my love for others?

How do I like others to show their love for me?

Do I have any friends that I'm worried about right now?

If I was in my friend's situation, what advice would I want to hear?

What do I think about most during the day?

What keeps me awake at night?

What do I think about politics?

Is being able to vote important to me?

What should schools teach more of?

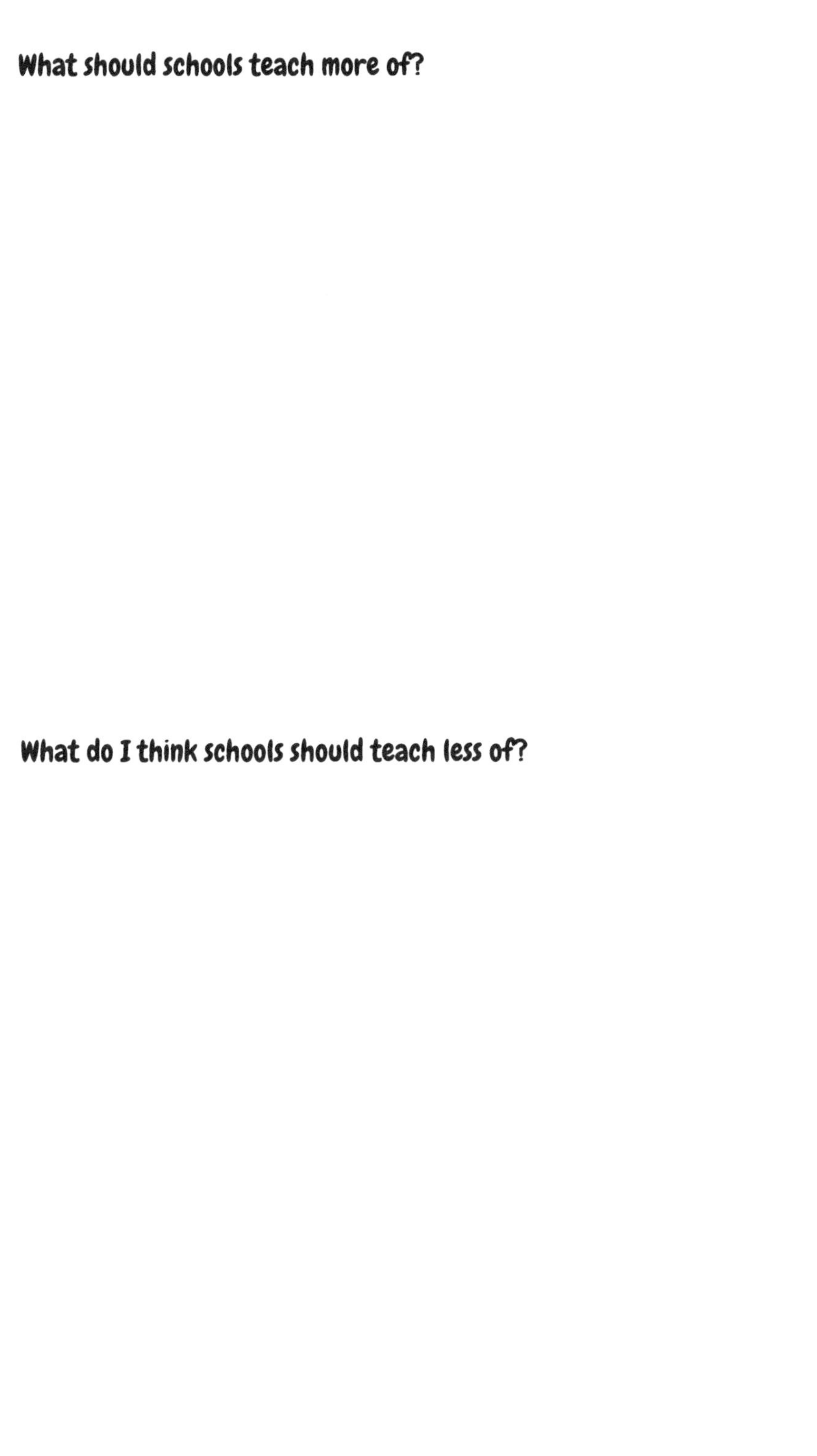

What do I think schools should teach less of?

My favorite things to do with my friends...

Do I ever feel jealous? How do I handle those feelings?

How important is having kids to me?

Is it ever ok to lie?

Do I have any bad or annoying habits?

What historic event do I wish I had been at or been part of?

If I could invite 3 people, alive or dead, to dinner, who would they be and why?

My earliest memory...

What 3 experiences have impacted my life so far?
Have they changed me for the better or worse?

Do I hold myself back? Are these obstacles real or imagined?

How often do I jump to conclusions?

Am I a leader or a follower?

What makes me feel empowered?

Have I ever been in an unhealthy relationship?
Did anyone try to warn me? How did I respond?

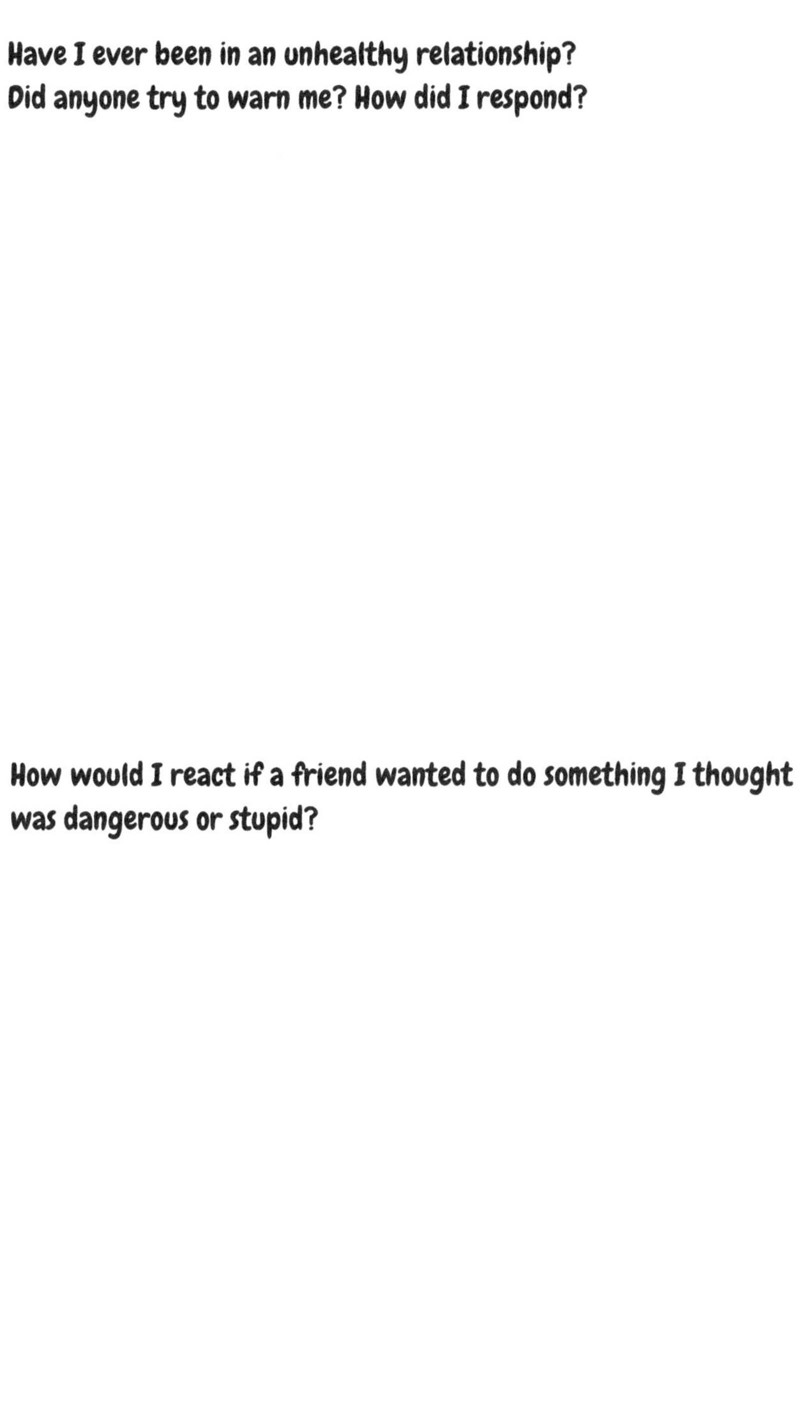

How would I react if a friend wanted to do something I thought
was dangerous or stupid?

How would I want to be remembered?
Am I being that person now?

Am I always kind?

Someone has just offered me a bus to convert into my own personal hangout space. Describe what I would do to make it into the perfect space for me...

What happens when we die?

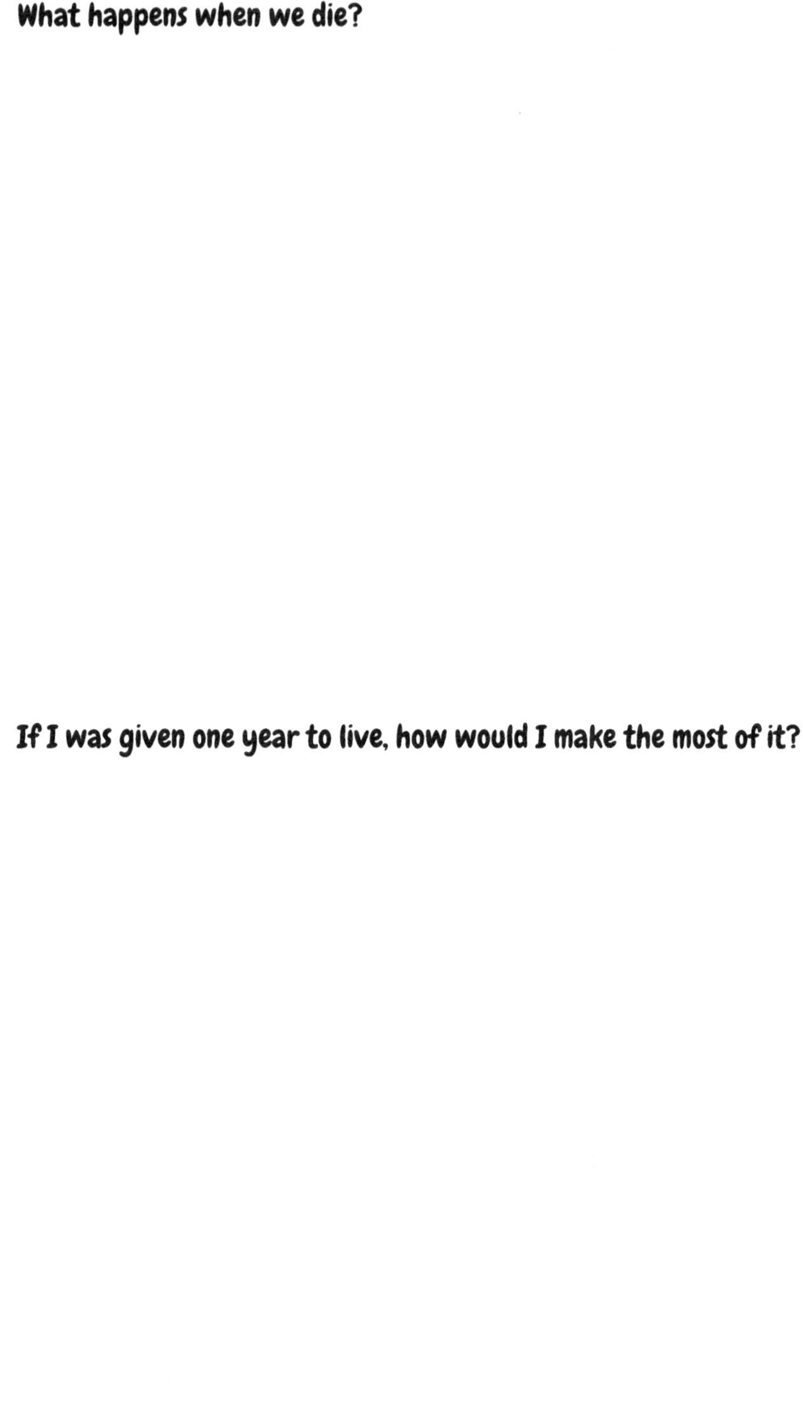

If I was given one year to live, how would I make the most of it?

Would I rather run my own business or work for someone else?

If I could give every person in the world the same gift, what would it be?

When my best friend is stressed, this is the advice I give them...

Am I kinder to my friends than I am myself? Why is that?
How could I be kinder to myself?

When does a teenager become an adult?

Of all the things I've learned, what do I think will be most useful
as an adult?

What is my greatest strength?

What is my greatest weakness?
How could I turn this into a strength?

Find a photograph or picture of people from a magazine and write a fictional story about them...

Find a photograph or picture of people from a magazine and write a fictional story about them...

If I knew I could live forever, what would I change about my life?

What is keeping me from complete happiness?

Can money buy happiness? Why or why not?

If I could be famous, what would I be famous for?

What do I think my clothes say about me?

What would be the funniest thing to fill a piñata with?

If we experience our greatest moments of growth and learning from failure, why are we so afraid to fail?

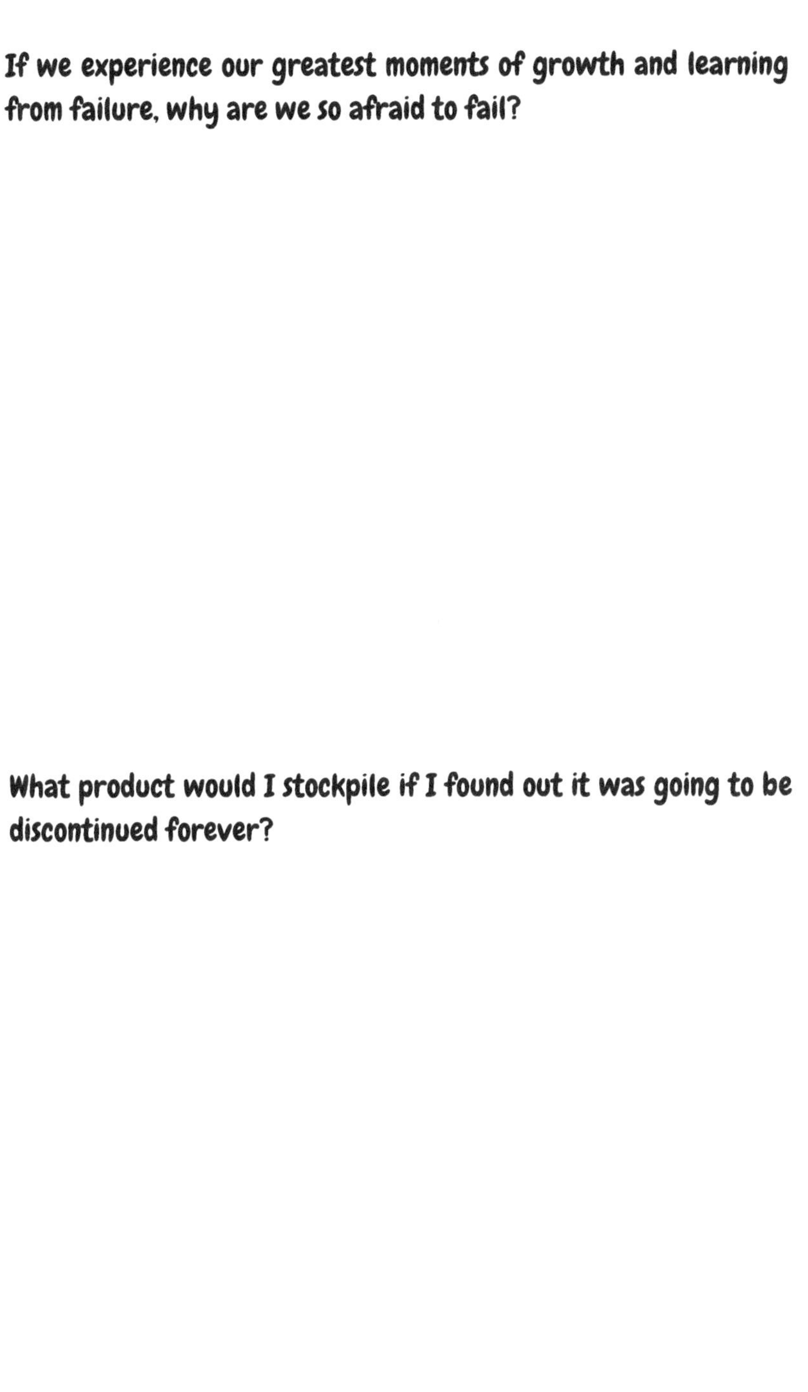

What product would I stockpile if I found out it was going to be discontinued forever?

Write out mixtape playlists for different people or occasions...

Write out mixtape playlists for different people or occasions...

My favorite app...

My favorite catchphrase...

If I had to replace my hands with household objects, what would I choose?

My favorite joke...

If I could trade places with someone for one day, who would it be?

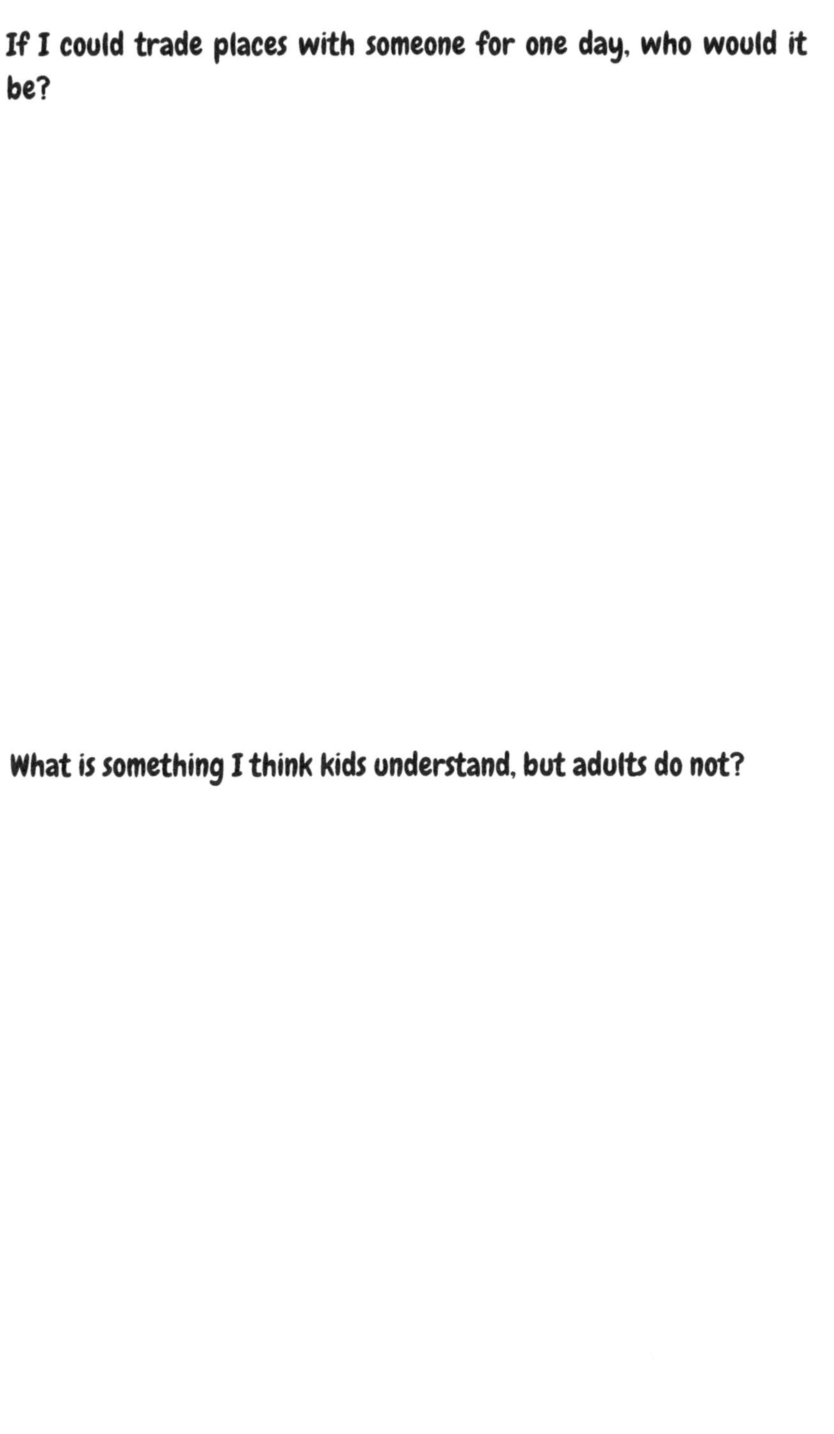

What is something I think kids understand, but adults do not?

What are my superstitions?

If I was going to bury a time capsule, what would I put in it?

What would my personal mascot be?

If I could learn the answer to one question about my future, what would it be?

Do I like the age I am now, or do I wish I was older/younger?
Why?

What is something I'm obsessed with?

This page is a collection of my favorite quotes...

Would I rather be able to teleport anywhere, or be able to read minds?

If I could say sorry to one person in history, who would it be and why?

Who would the best person to be stuck in an elevator with be?

Who would be the worst person to be stuck in an elevator with be?

A list of all the most memorable events of my past...

If I could ask 3 celebrities any question, who would I ask and what would the question be?

If I was famous, how would I use my fame to help others?

What was the last disagreement I had and who was it with?

How could I have handled it better?

Have I ever wanted to be popular?

Who are my heroes and what qualities do I admire in them?

If I could travel back in time 3 years, what advice would I write to myself in a letter?

Do I ever feel lonely or left out? If yes, how could I change this?

What hurts my feelings?

What is my darkest secret?

If someone trusted me with a big secret, would I tell anyone?

What will the world look like in 25 years time?

What is really important to me now, that will still be important in 25 years?

5 of the worst experiences of my life so far...

5 things I would never do again...

5 things I've always wanted to do but haven't done yet...

The 5 best times in my life so far...

Someone whose company I enjoy . . .

Someone who I admire . . .

Something I am proud of . . .

Who do I talk to when I have a problem? How do they help?

If I could live anywhere in the world, where would it be? Why?

IF I could have 3 wishes, what would they be?

What do I wish my friends knew about me?

What do I wish my parents knew about me?

What do I feel ashamed of?

Where do I feel safest?

Write a letter to someone I love, saying all the things I've been meaning to say for years... I don't have to send it!...

If I wasn't afraid, what would I do?

What does failure mean to me?
Have I ever felt like a failure? How did I cope?

How can I tell that I'm getting angry?
Where do I feel it in my body? What does it feel like?

How am I unique?

What's something that adults have said to me that's really stuck?
Are they right?

What do I do when people don't seem to like me?

What things are in my control? What is out of my control?
How does it feel to notice that some things are out of my control?

In my control	Out of my control

What do I do when I'm stressed out? How do I calm myself down?

What is something nice that I could say to myself?

What do I do when I'm feeling down?

Who is my oldest friend? How did we meet?
How do they make me feel?

Who is my newest friend? How did we meet?
How do they make me feel?

What qualities do I offer as a friend?

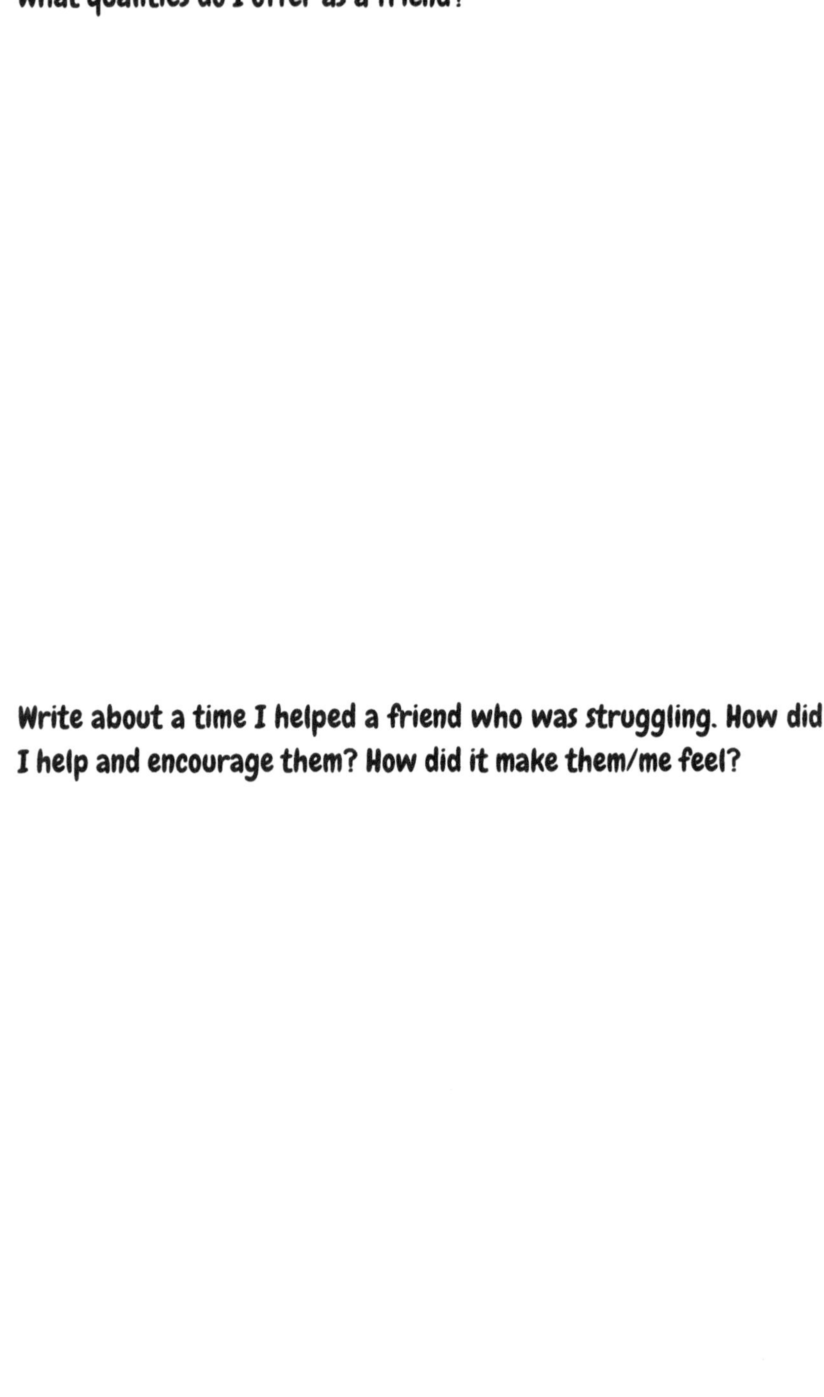

Write about a time I helped a friend who was struggling. How did I help and encourage them? How did it make them/me feel?

A new life skill that I have learned recently...

What is one way I would like my friends/family/siblings to work or play better together?

What is the toughest challenge I've experienced in the last year? How did I overcome it? What did I learn?

When is a time that I felt really powerful?
How can I use my power to help others?

What do I take for granted (ie running water)?

Who do I take for granted?

What worries me most about the future?

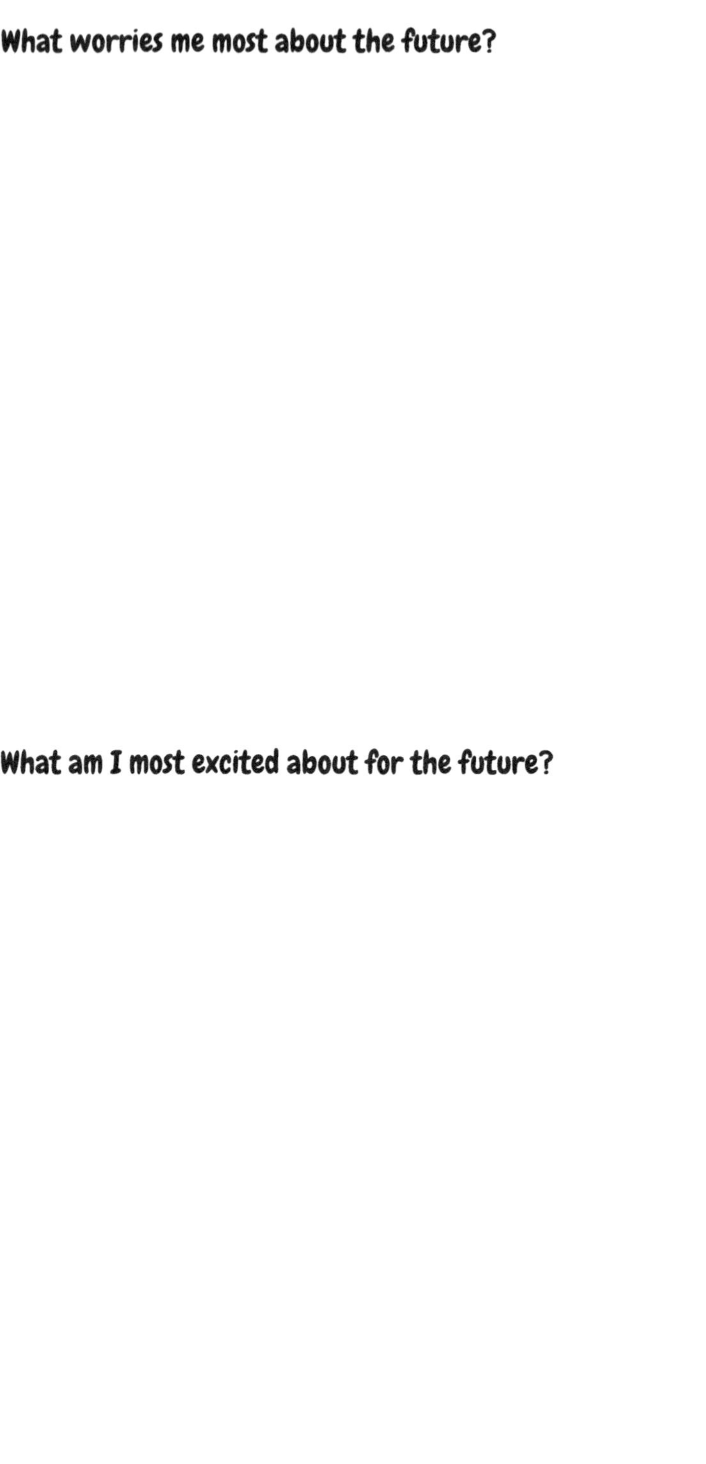

What am I most excited about for the future?

What matters most in my life?

Which is worse, failing or never trying?

Am I holding on to something I need to let go of?

Does it really matter what people think of me?

I couldn't imagine living life without...

What do I love about life?

What is one thing I wish I'd done but didn't because I was afraid?

What is one thing I wish I had never done?

5 things I like about myself...

Which 3 words describe me best? Ask friends to use one word to describe me, do their words match mine?

What excites me?

When I'm feeling down, how do I cheer myself up?

Write about a time when I felt wronged by someone. If this happened again now, would my reaction be the same?

Do I need to forgive someone? Write them a letter explaining how they made me feel and how I've forgiven them (I don't need to send it!)

Who can I never forgive? Why not?

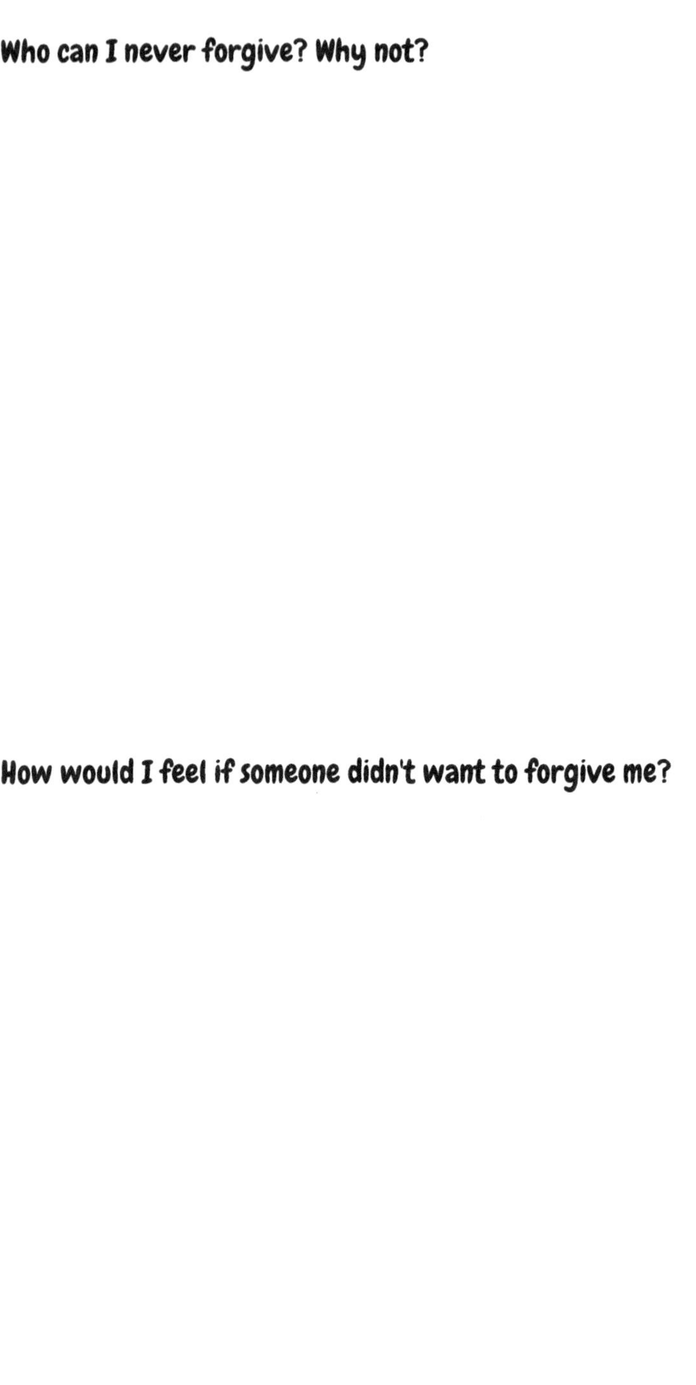

How would I feel if someone didn't want to forgive me?

What do I need to forgive myself for?

On a scale of 1-10, how happy am I with my life right now?
What can I today to improve my score?

How do I handle anger and frustration?
Is there a better way to deal with it?

What does my ideal day look like?

Create a mood board of words, quotes and images of the person I want to become...

If I won the lottery tomorrow, what would I do with the money?

If money was no object, what would I do all day?

What is something I'd love to learn?

What is my most treasured memory?

Never have I ever...

- [ ] Been kissed
- [ ] Pretended to be someone famous
- [ ] Licked a dog
- [ ] Cried in public
- [ ] Sung in the shower
- [ ] Been pooped on by a bird
- [ ] Drunk too much alcohol
- [ ] Played Spin the Bottle
- [ ] Forged a signature
- [ ] Lied to my parents/caregiver about where I was going
- [ ] Broken a bone
- [ ] Stayed up all night
- [ ] Been on TV
- [ ] Recorded a video of myself singing and/or dancing
- [ ] Stolen money from a parent/caregiver
- [ ] Pretended to be sick to miss school
- [ ] Had a crush on a teacher
- [ ] Failed a test
- [ ] Laughed so much I peed my pants
- [ ] Hidden food under my bed

Who would I like to have a better relationship with?
What is stopping this from happening?

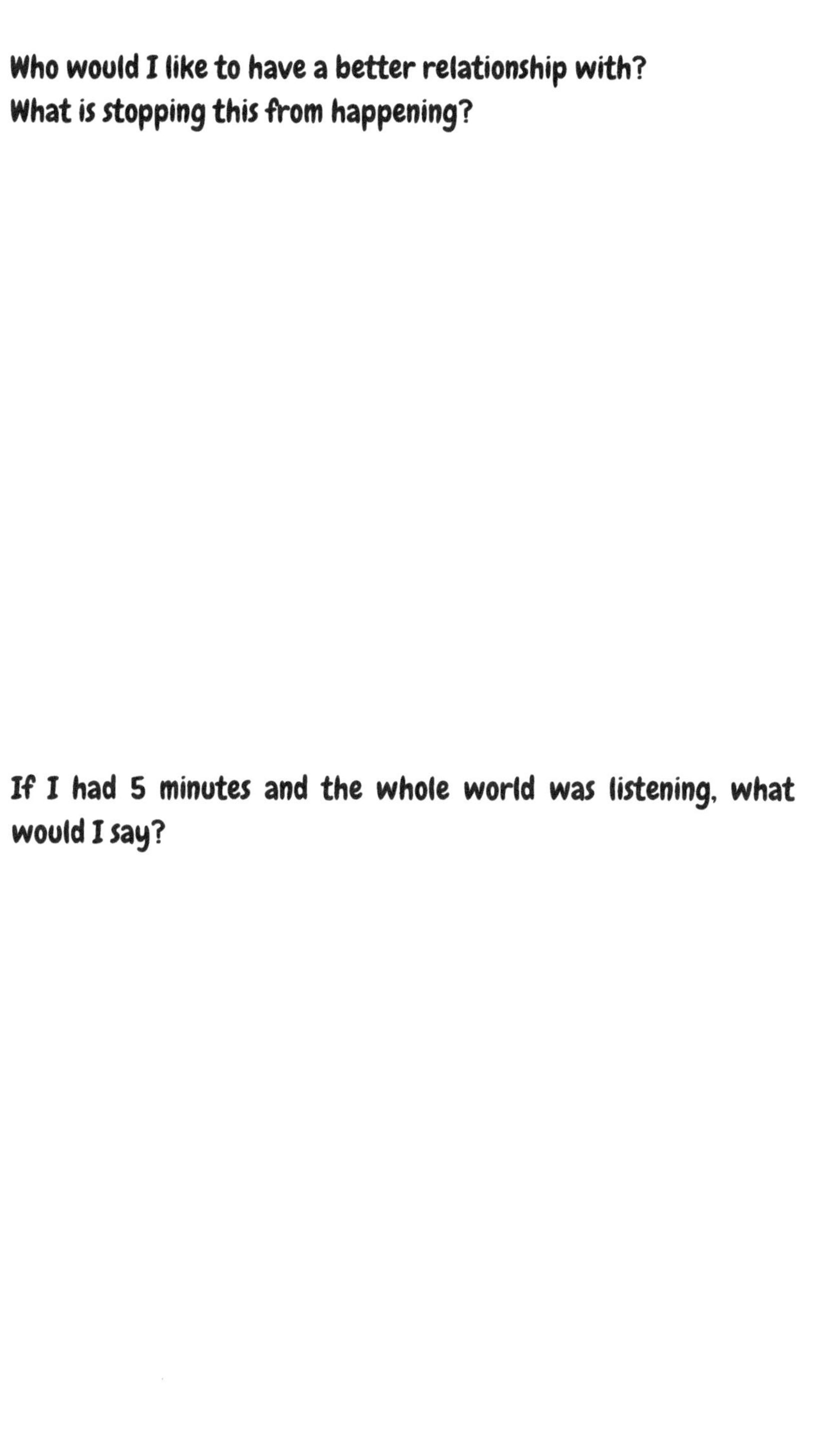

If I had 5 minutes and the whole world was listening, what would I say?

How similar am I to my parents?

What is the nicest thing someone has ever told me?

Who is my best friend? What makes them special?

What does being a good friend mean to me?
Am I this person to others?

Who do I have a really good relationship with?
What makes this/these relationships special?

What do people misunderstand about me? Why is that?

When was the last time I was disappointed? What part did I play? What could have happened differently to avoid disappointment?

Am I hard on myself sometimes? Is this reaction justified?

What do I need help with? Am I confident in asking for help?
If not, why not?

What is something I'd like to improve about myself?
What do I need to start doing this?

A list of things I'm good at...

Would I rather live for a week in the past, or in the future? Why?

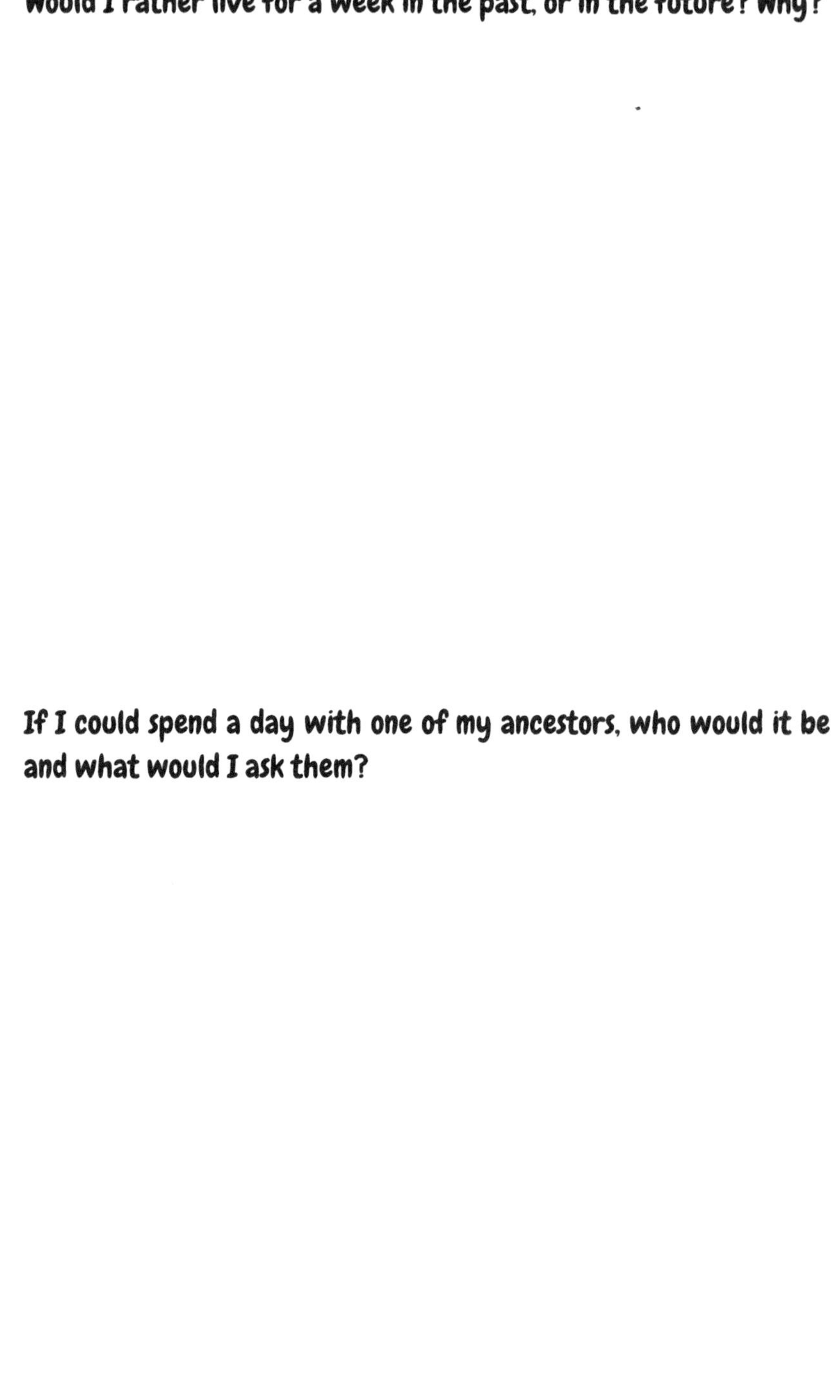

If I could spend a day with one of my ancestors, who would it be and what would I ask them?

If I could travel through time, where would I go?

If I could live in any TV home, what would it be?

What was my favorite childhood toy?

What is my most embarrassing childhood memory?

Write a goodbye letter to someone or something...

What was my favorite childhood vacation?

What was my favorite childhood book or story?

Bucket List...

During my lifetime I want to...

If I could only eat 3 foods for the rest of my life, what would they be?

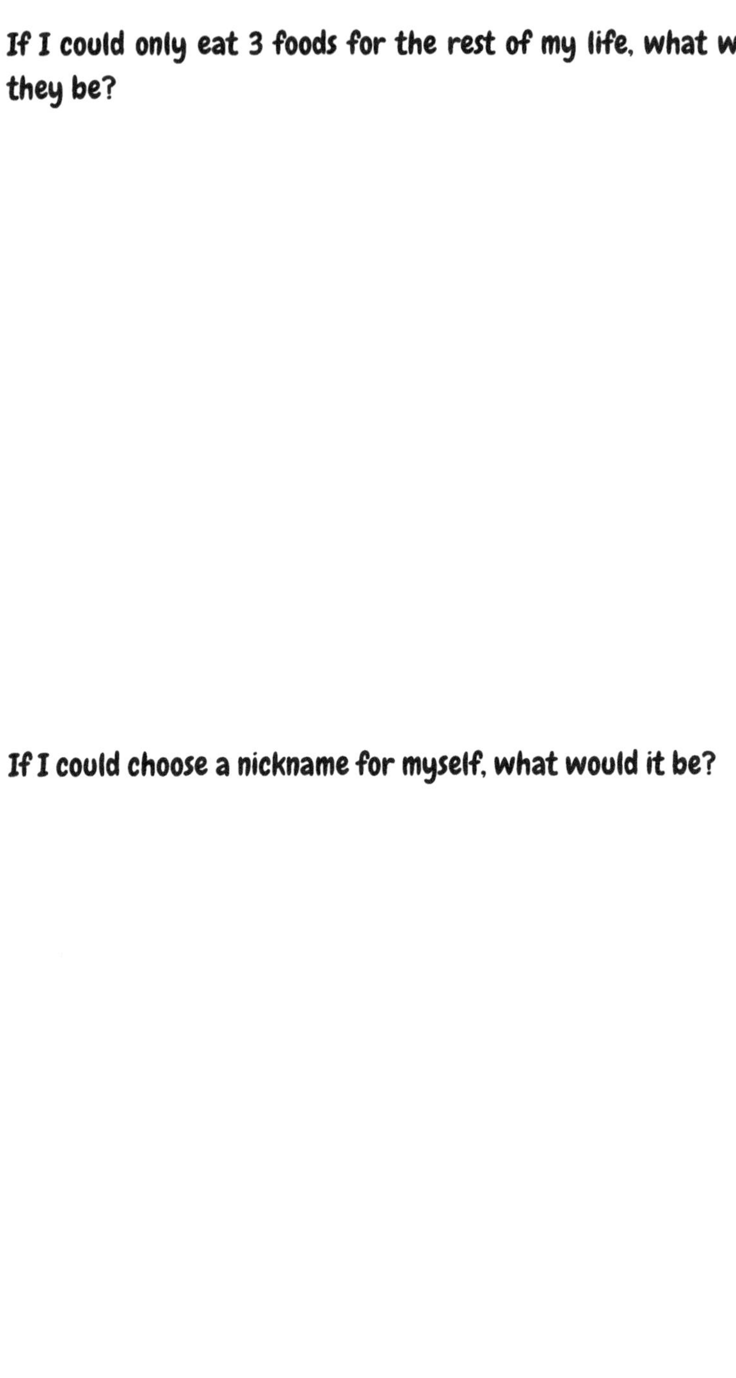

If I could choose a nickname for myself, what would it be?

Who is the funniest person I know?

What makes me laugh?

Create a painting of my mood right now. What colors have I used and why?

What is my favorite movie quote?

What is my favorite family tradition?

When a friend is having a bad day, how do I make them feel better?

Using one word, how would I describe my family?

What trait do I like most about myself?

What is the best piece of advice I've ever received?

Who is my celebrity crush?

If someone made a movie of my life, who would play the main characters?

What is the worst thing I did as a kid?

What was a time I got into big trouble with my parents?

What would I do in life if I knew I could never fail?

What is the best part of being part of my family?

What is the weirdest thing I've ever eaten?

Does my name have a special meaning and/or was I named after someone special?

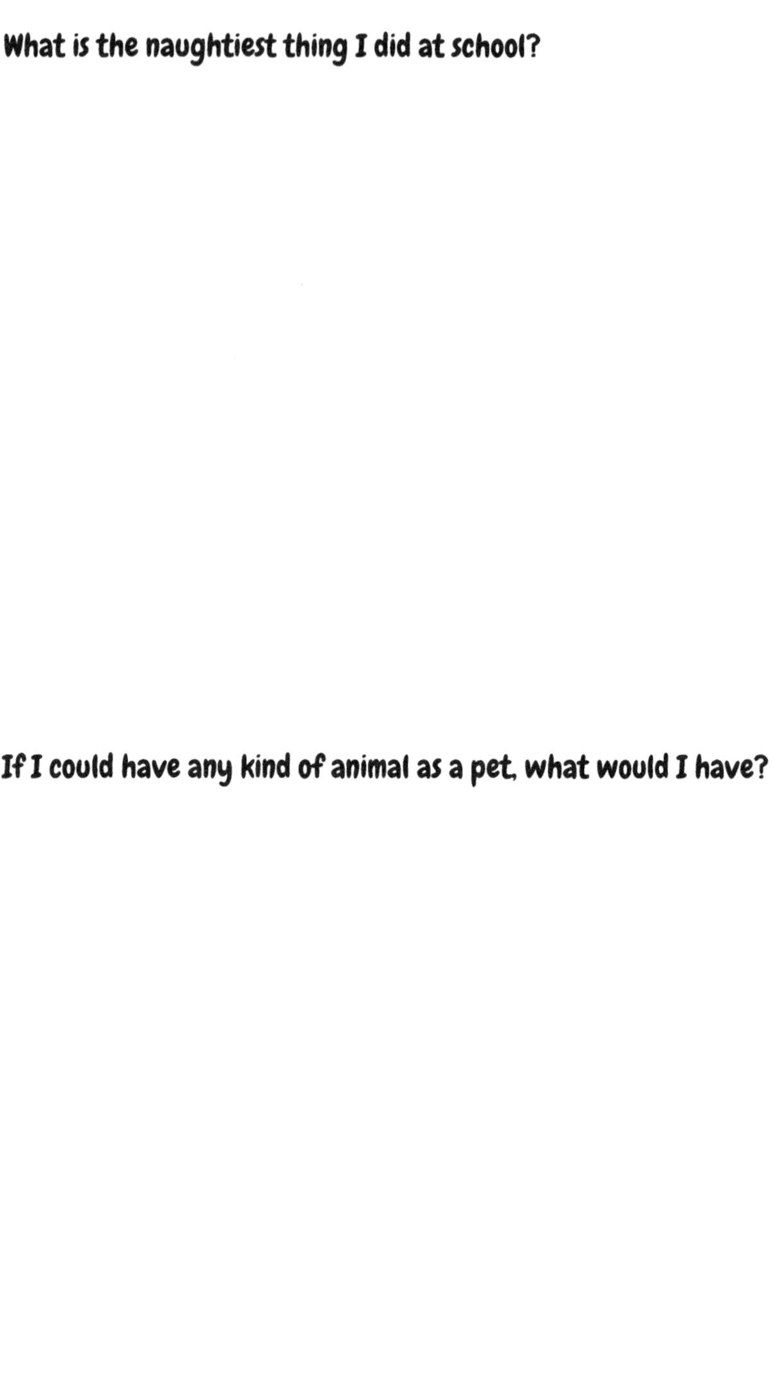

What is the naughtiest thing I did at school?

If I could have any kind of animal as a pet, what would I have?

What is the hardest thing I have ever done?

What is the most beautiful thing I have ever seen in nature?

What is the most terrifying situation I've ever been in?
What did I learn from it?

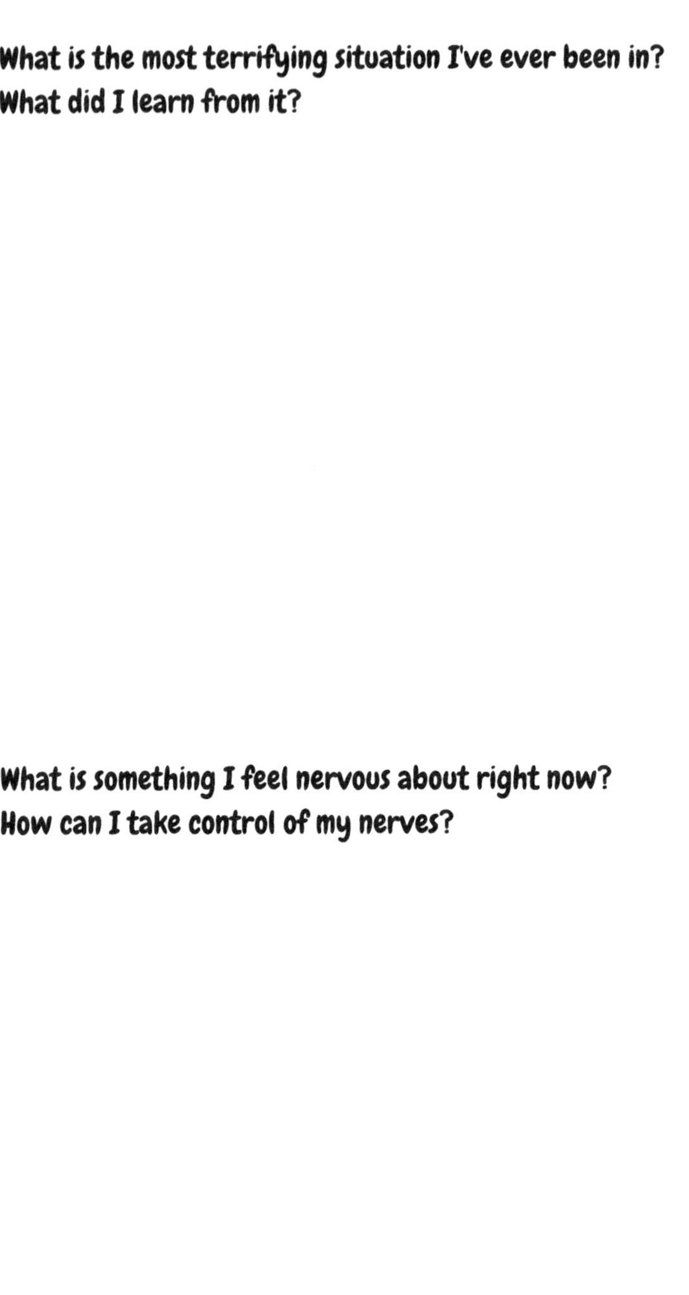

What is something I feel nervous about right now?
How can I take control of my nerves?

I get mad when...

Who do I trust the most and why?

Which bad habits of other people drive me crazy?

Do I have a weird or funny habit that no one knows about?

How do I think others view me? Why is that?

What is one fun fact about me?

In my opinion, this is the best song ever written and this is how it makes me feel... Write or stick in the lyrics...

If I could change 3 things about the world, what would I change and why?

What motivates me the most?

What does love mean to me?

What do I want my life to look like in 5 years? In 10 years?

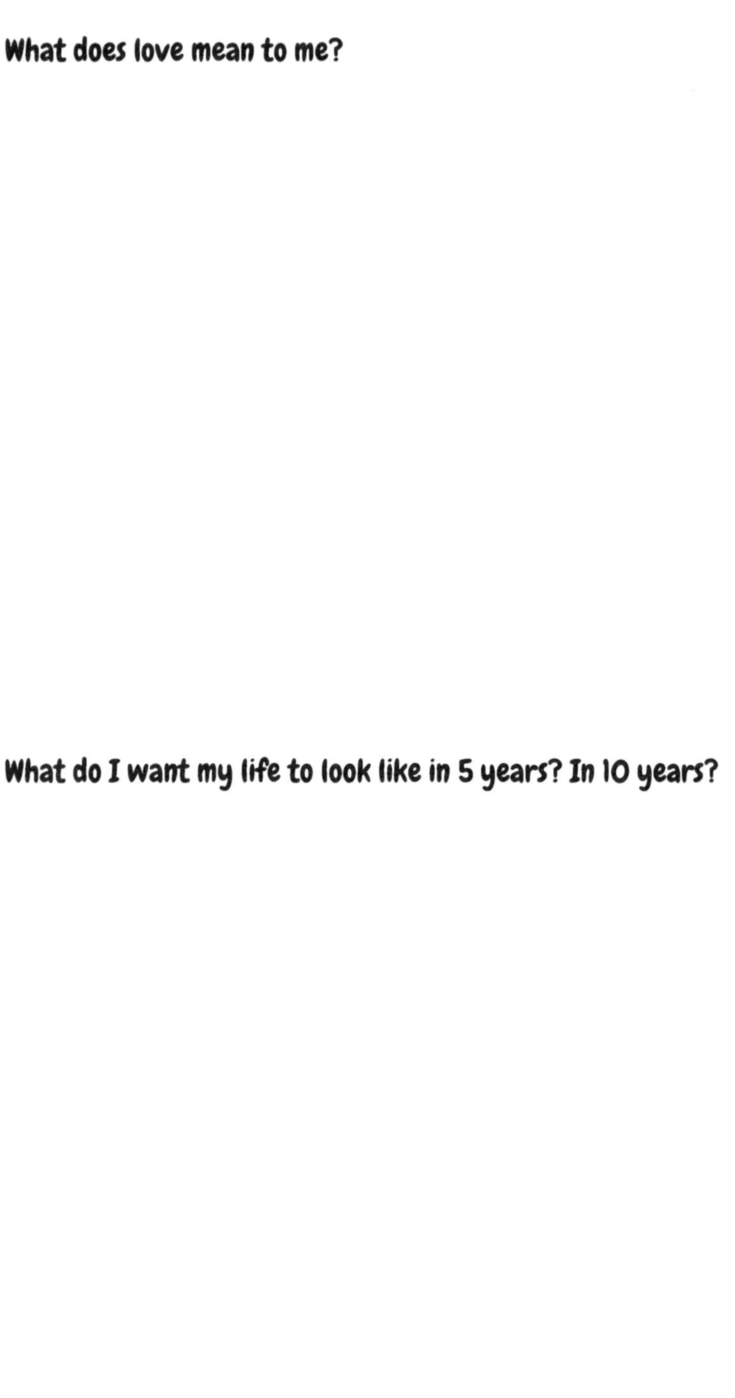

What is one thing my parents do now that I will never do when I have kids?

Have I ever wanted to run away from home? Tell the story...

Write a poem or a song about something or someone that means a lot to you. It doesn't have to rhyme!

Who do I miss? Why are they no longer part of my life?

What do I wish I'd told someone before it was too late?

What effect do I think social media has on me and the people around me?

Do I act differently online than in real life?

What is my secret desire?

What is the biggest lie I've ever told?

Write a letter to my future self...

A valuable lesson I learned...

A fun experience I had...

3 celebrities I admire...

3 celebrities I think are lame...

What relaxes me?

What makes me happy?

An unexpected good thing that happened...

I'm grateful for my friendship with   because...

When I feel the urge to pick up my phone, I'm going to open this book instead and describe what I was going to do on my phone..

Favorite memory of my mother/female caregiver...

Favorite memory of my father/male caregiver...

5 things I love about my home...

5 things I love about my country...

Who has taught me the most in life?

Who do I admire? What qualities in them do I admire?

Favorite subject at school... Why was this my favorite?

Favorite teacher... What did they teach? Why did I like them?

My favorite secret location and why... stick in a photo or draw it...

My favorite person... stick in a photo or draw them...

When was the last time I helped someone out?

Who should I have said thank you to recently?

3 things that make me feel better when I am ill...

3 favorite comfort foods...

What are the good aspects of social media?

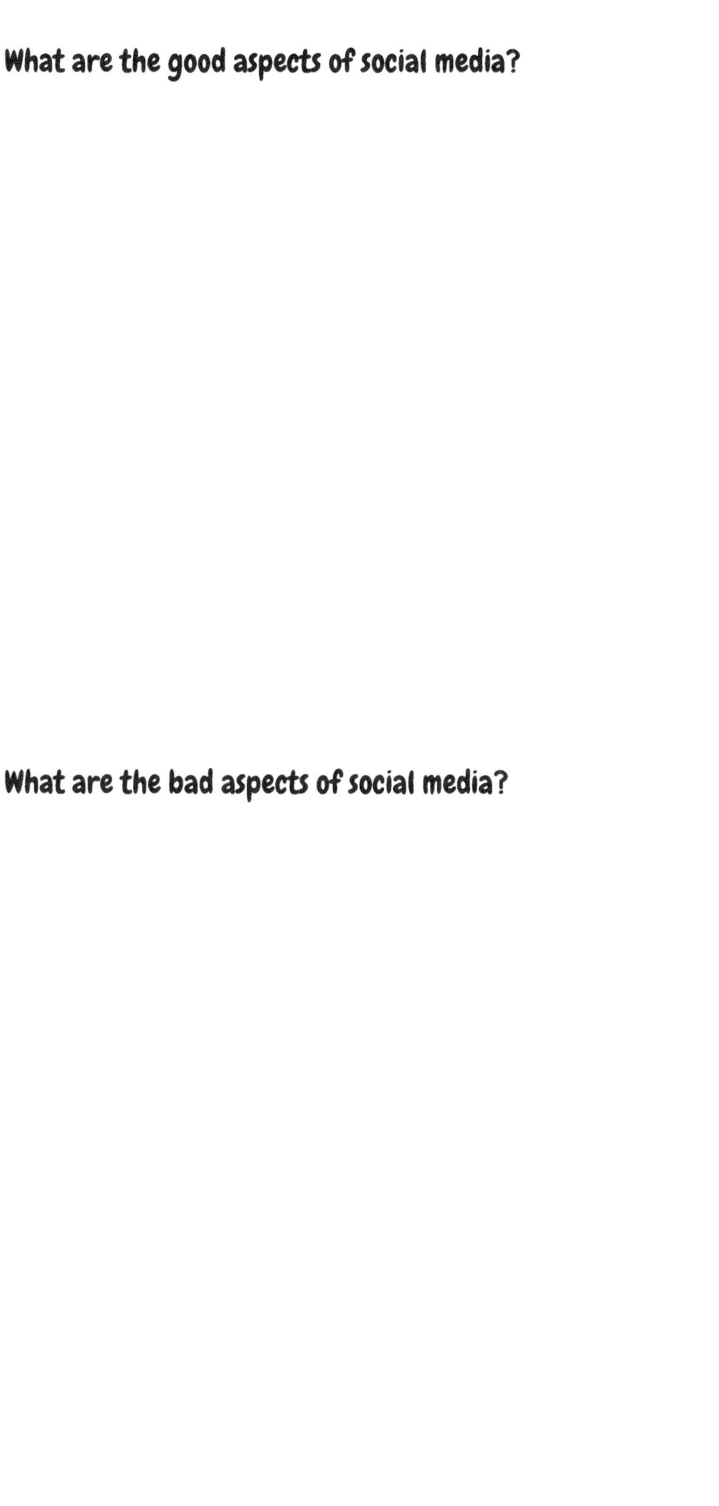

What are the bad aspects of social media?

How can I do better tomorrow?

How can I help someone tomorrow?

List and doodle things I'm grateful for...

My favorite shop and why...

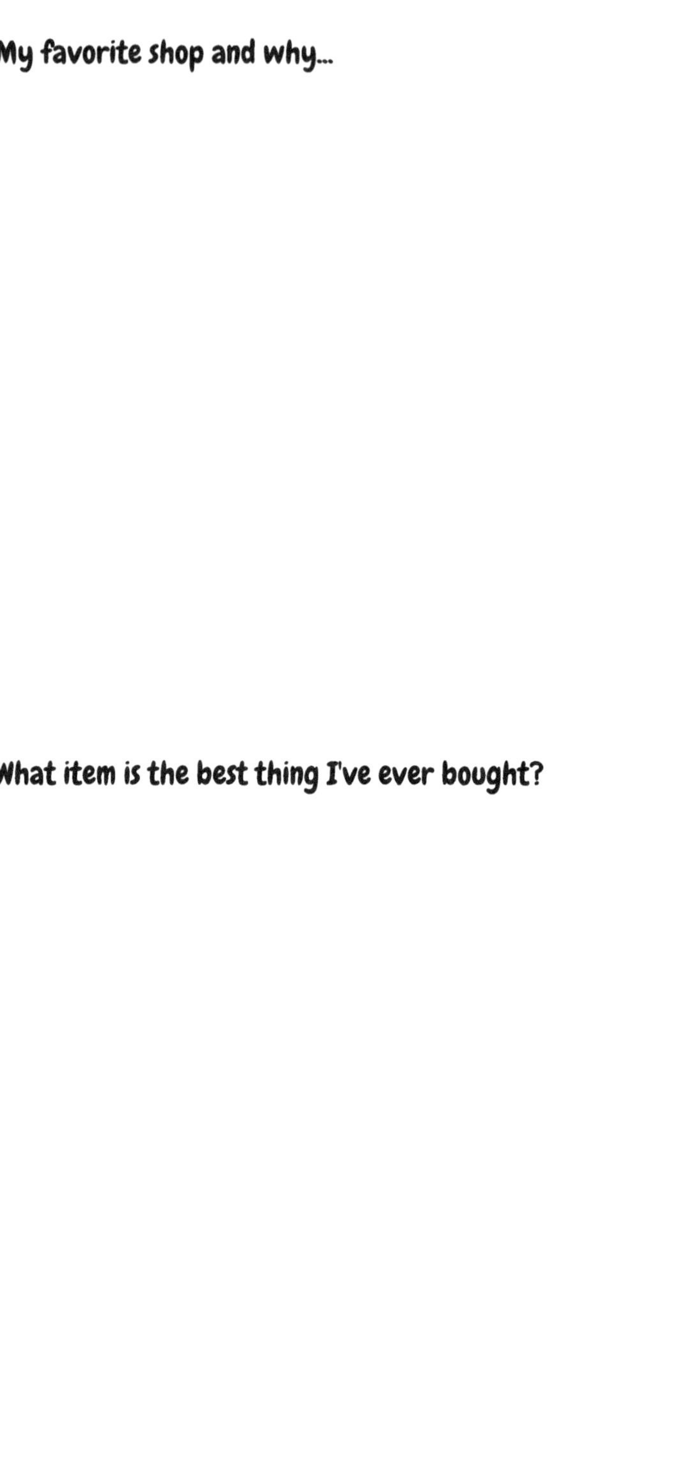

What item is the best thing I've ever bought?

A time I was unlucky...

A time I was lucky...

My 5 favorite songs...

My 5 favorite dinners...

My 5 favorite books...

My 5 favorite movies...

30 things that make me smile...

My favorite smell...

My favorite sound...

5 items that are really important to me...

5 items I could live without...

This would be the soundtrack to my life...

My future in 3 words...

My past in 3 words...

Lasts...

Pet...

School...

Friend...

Best friend...

Hobby...

Party...

Sleepover...

Love...

Kiss...

Fight...

More Lasts...

Performance...

Time I helped a friend...

Song I downloaded...

Live band...

Vacation overseas...

Significant event in history I can remember...

Proud of myself moment...

Time I felt embarrassed...

Item I bought...

Time I realised I was good at something...

Right now I am...

Listening...

Reading...

Making...

Feeling...

Planning...

Loving...

About the Author

Ali lives in the stunning South West of England with her tweenage son, Jack, Pharaoh the labradoodle and cats Lexi and Bailey.

Following a few years of life's trials and tribulations Ali became a mid life coach, specialising in transforming women over the age of 40 from worriers into warriors. Becoming a coach helped her discover her purpose, who she is, what ignites her soul, what fulfils her and what inspires her - helping other women to find these forgotten attributes in themselves, guiding them in rediscovering their super powers and helping to dust off their capes!

As part of her coaching journey Ali has created several books and journals for children, teenagers and adults themed around gratitude, wellbeing, self-exploration and reflection .

Ali has a weakness for Reece's Peanut Buttercups.